Robins
and Other
Messengers

A Spring Journal

Poems by Patrick Simpson
Drawings by Janene Roberts

Robins and Other Messengers
by Patrick Simpson
with drawings by Janene Roberts

© 2009 by Patrick Simpson
Printed in the United States of America by Wordsprint,
        Christiansburg, Virginia

ISBN 978-0-926487-44-4

To
Jana Ruble,
my wife and dear friend,
whose imagination and love of reading
created the idea for this book.

The poems, with their designated dates in
chronological order, constitute a lyrical journal
of the season of late winter
through mid-spring of the year 2008.

March 10

I

Push open a door into the March afternoon, now
Hear the air pulsing with
Peaceful rocking
Bird melody, of
Sweetness, sturdiness;
Steady and halting, bravely
Ancient and generous, in turn
A blessing, a lesson,
A Madonna allowing
Embrace of the child within.

How reverent now this late winter sun, spreading
Strongly, while caressing a
Colorless earth
Encompassing this song,
Expressing imperturbable
Love.

March 13

II

Wind threads through the yard like a dull Chinook:
It doesn't belong here,
Tell the robins and
Tell them it never rains enough any more.
Warmth and wind:
Clothes dry quickly on the line.
And I feel deeply sad
Crocuses and all.

Birds fluttered aimlessly, songs were
Rusty and grating, sporatic.
I felt the sweetness would return somehow
With the sound of thunder
Tomorrow.

March 15

III

Sometimes it feels as if there are
Only broken pieces
And the confines of the walls, like the
Overcast and damp evening
Close in and crush the spirit.
Then, from the door, pushed again into the evening,
I listen to the sharp bird notes, here,
Across the way,
Beyond the tall spruce spires,
Sturdy, with no anger, no
Accusation that anything is other than
Completely whole.

This points toward the space
Between galaxies.

March 19
IV

Almost all chill is wrung from the
Evening air. It's
Dark now, almost muggy.
Bird melodies, robins and their
Concert allies, expressive phrases
Echo, and reverberate through my
Mind's hallways.
Here are doors through which I might
Pass, push them open like my
Front door with the glass
Letting me breathe in the
Familiar haunting fragrance that
March now provides.

These cycles are not like what I think:
I do not understand the messages
The way I thought I had.

March 19
V

I could not hear the sparrow sing
Beyond the back door.
He skimmed along the porch
Under the feeders, so fragile.
Was a foot crippled?
The rain had let up.
A tiny streaked body, safe:
The squirrels and larger birds
Absent; the present moment now
Completely serene,

Completely at rest, ready
To roost the night in a woody crotch
Safe from wind and thunder:
A spirit at ease.

March 21
VI

A Good Friday moonlight
Silver-coats houses, walkways, branches,
Havens of robins with closed eyes, not
Shivering for survival tonight:
In blessed mildness
Contradicting the age-old storm of
Crucifixion.
A night of boundless atonement
And rest.

I invite the songs of the
Sleeping birds to merge with my
Dreams of beneficent dawn.

March 21
VII

Iridescent doves, rapidly
Carry assigned
Messages of grace, Ethereal
Whirrings, scarcely audible
Linking our hearts with theirs:
Seeming to float from the airy
Realms that can never completely
Belong to our bodies. They belong to
Vibrant worlds of sunlight, and to
Mysterious dazzling moments of
White bloodroot blossoms,
Astonishing amidst the decay of
Winter.

Listen now.
Listen with our hearts!

March 22
VIII

To return to that same nook
In the garden, by the south wall, now
Just to plant a new rose,
Replace a hollyhock, in the
Shadows of roses long perished
Where the wrens flutter and scamper with
Beaks full of leaves gathered for
This year's nest.
In that very yard by the same gate,
Generations of new songs, blatant and
Shamelessly exuberant
Renewing a mystical task, a covenant
As sure as unveiling the statues
In church, tearing aside purple grief.

Could it all change in an instant
With a new rose, a new breath, savored?
Ah, love that is song and watered dirt.

March 26
IX

Twilight bird choruses tonight shimmer in
Layers; tree shadows deepen.
Voices call out: discussing
Roosting havens, tree crotch and branch,
Water in the birdbath,
This patch of grass,
This port on the old feeder.
Life-energy flows, interacts, bird with
Tree with the air, with wind,
With my presence by the watering can,
The same back yard, a
Day of warmth.

Layers of tranquility undulate
Like rippled waters in the bath:
A lone robin splashes.

March 31

X.

Walking the hills,
The neighborhood streets
Breathing in the foggy dampness,
Filling myself with the strange
Fading night-glow
With bird music counterpointed from
Every direction.
Their emotions and mine
Are fused in blunt old rock,
Worn down ridges
In this glimmering space where
We briefly share this hidden valley.

I return home in the dark,
The work in the garden is done.

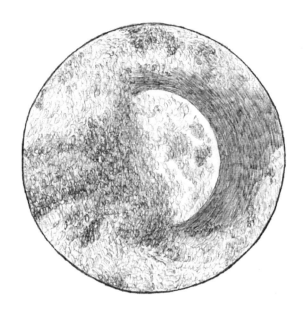

April 6
XI.

I understand neither quick thoughts nor fears.
From the front door there is
Darkness and fog. I don't want to walk away into it:
Not for a few minutes.
The weather forecasters predict
A week of cloudiness and fog, but no rain.
They are always wrong.

Finally sadness is absent.
Analytical, quicksilver me is worn out of
Flying away like messenger birds.
It is unbearable in the fog.
I would huddle with them in the fir branches,
In deep bird sleep,
With infinite expectation of dawn:

It is desire to be forever young, this
Listening to the wood-thrush.

April 10
XII

Chatter of robins sounds like
Rusty gates:
Then the liquid, lyrical rocking
Blends into the night, melts into
First quarter moonlight with its
Muted shadows cast, then
All the birds are stone.

I remain in the shadowy space
But the neighbor dogs
Bark like crashing dishes:
Likely they see a groundhog.
I move
Inside with closed windows. Still I feel the

Fresh air and I breathe in the turmoil:
China, Tibet, Iraq:
I breathe out the flowing avian lyrics.

April 11
XIII

Friday, late, familiar: endless weeping of
Distant sirens.
Restless, excitement-seeking youths
Crowd weekend streets
Downtown, a mile away:
Mourning Doves roost touching
Thick spruce branches, just beyond my
Bedroom window. I recall old, old feelings:
I would return late to my driveway and
Company of sleeping
Titmice, cardinals: oblivious to
Prowling, garnet owl eyes.

Night wind tugs at inner door latches,
Then, my thoughts were calm.
The world was safely complex.
The seasons had not begun to unravel,
The garden seemed safe. There were storms

And lightning glared down the hallway,
Reflected in the glass of cupboards,
Suggested a walk on the
Path in the nearby woods.
There was a wild space full of
Straight tulip trees, flanked by
Slashes of briars.

And there was snow to dream about,
And the virgin pines and hemlocks.

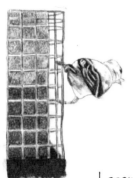

April 12
XIV

I scan the feeders, late morning:
Nuthatches dart,
A solitary sparrow sits
Nibbling, joined by fellow finches,
Brilliant. There is a veiled sun
Eternally happy.
Rhythmical wind tosses the
Many branches, some fresh with new green;
I breathe from an open window
some energetic vapor as
Many birds cluster, little packages of
Joy, color, vitality.

My thoughts want to fly, and desire hovers,
But for now I am free.

April 13
XV

Near midnight, snowing softly,
I imagine inches
Accumulate on high ridges.
The storm is small.
Quietly I forgive
Disappearance of the great snows,
Surely one of the
Most difficult tests of my life.

Up the hill, dozens of newly planted
Trees feel the moisture's chill
Fingers. There will be new havens.

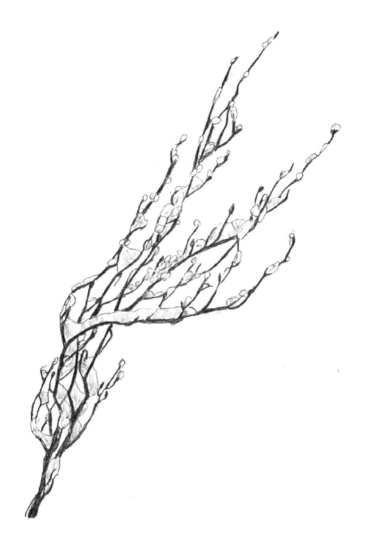

April 15
XVI.

This night's moonlight is more invasive,
Wants to wriggle through branches of
Shrubs just outside, pass through
Unexpected windows, enter never touched corners
And grow immense, like
Strange daylight. Pours down
Like questions posed
You didn't really expect
Answered. Precious now is the richness,
Like the rose, like the bloodroot.

Stillness also, but not in the way
You expected.
No, you think, that isn't what
I thought I had to get.
Not at all. Not at all.

April 16
XVII

And the meanings in the songs come:
One by one
Directly, without words, only
Buds, blossoms, a fragrance:
Peeling bark on a slender trunk, a
Place of solace.
You smile at yourself
And the moon as your now messenger,
A clear mirror, an entrance. A sigh.
Tears fall, not betraying anything.
Freedom. Where the blessings end.
The late cardinal finishes the aria.
You don't have to understand the language.
There is
Only an indecipherable message read
In the heart.

I have written poetry periodically throughout my life. Reading and writing, along with sports and being out-doors, especially in the mountains, have consumed much of my passion. I was schooled to be a performer on the cello and double bass, and was employed as a college professor. I retired from teaching at Virginia Tech after thirty years. Before moving to Blacksburg, I taught at colleges in Louisiana, Illinois, and Colorado.

Patrick Simpson, M.Mus.

I have been on the faculty of the Department of Interdis-ciplinary Studies at Virginia Tech for twenty years, teach-ing humanities courses such as The Creative Process and Introduction to Humanities and the Arts. My own love of gardens made me respond strongly to the images and feelings in Patrick's poems. Drawing these images has increased my intimacy with these natural wonders.

Janene Roberts, Ph.D.

What a pleasure to see this beautiful lyric diary of spring fly forth in March. Robins and Other Messengers, by Patrick Simpson, is both a cycle of poems and delicate, feathery sketches of the creatures that return in spring. Janene Roberts' pen and ink imagery gives the book a breath of its own. A visionary uniqueness. Her moon-bird, the wooden garden gate, the front door to a home, each invite the reader into the approach of another season. Many of Simpson's evoc... seem to have a sonnet "turn" the reader's attention, and del... Such as "no accusation, no anger (here), only wholeness . . . space between galaxies." What an effective leap and seeming contradiction! A song of "water and dirt," spring is. Step into this small biome of words that, as the poet declares, is "bravely ancient and generous." You will spend the day and discover the way in which language can, indeed, refresh. Re-ignite.

— Katherine Soniat, author of A Shared Life

ISBN 0-926487-44-2

Published by Pocahontas Press, Inc.
Blacksburg, Virginia